THE

Wilderness
Companion

Compiled and with an Introduction by
David Backes

NORTHWORD
PRESS, INC
Box 1360, Minocqua, WI 54548

DEDICATION

To Jim Egan, S.J.
and
Rev. Tony McCarthy

Copyright ©1992 by David Backes
NorthWord Press, Inc.
P.O. Box 1360
Minocqua, WI 54548

Edited by Greg Linder
Designed by Russell S. Kuepper
Art created from photographs courtesy
Robert W. Baldwin and Tom Klein

Library of Congress Cataloging-in-Publication Data

Backes, David.
   A wilderness companion / David Backes.
      p.   cm.
   Includes bibliographical references.
   ISBN 1-55971-185-X
   1. Nature--Literary collections.   I. Title.
PN6071.N3B24   1992
082--dc20   92-24535
                                                         CIP

❖ CONTENTS ❖

❖ PREFACE ❖

Sigurd Olson once wrote that a longstanding habit of his on canoe trips was to take along little scraps of paper on which he'd copied brief passages taken from the writings of poets, saints, and other spiritual seekers. He would gather these bits of prose and poetry in what he called his "medicine bag," and now and then while he was in the canoe he'd pick one out, put it on the pack in front of him, anchor it with a stone, and slowly read it.

Like many others, Olson found that wilderness provides an ideal setting for reflection: "Paddling along watching the skies, clouds, and horizons, there is time to mull such thoughts deeply and translate them not in one's own mind, but in the timeless background of hills and distance, the eternal and the immutable." To Olson, wilderness travel and contemplation yielded spiritual benefits desperately needed in a Cold War culture that seemed to be teetering on the brink of nuclear annihilation.

The Cold War is now apparently over, but the spiritual restlessness that Olson recognized continues to be widespread. North American society is among the wealthiest on earth, but there is an inner poverty and longing that no amount of material success can quench. As much as any society in the world, ours promotes an ethic of self-realization, but the rising number of addiction-shattered lives testifies to our fundamental powerlessness. We have the world's best system of higher education, but its emphasis on analytical thought and measurement leaves us ill-prepared to answer the questions deep in our hearts, the questions that defy analysis and measurement.

At least partly in response to this internal bewilderment, millions of us retreat to wild places each year. Whether our trip is for a weekend or a week, many of us are making a spiritual pilgrimage. We seek an experience that adds meaning and perspective to our lives, but some of us hope for even more: We want to relieve our inner turmoil and brokenness, to admit our powerlessness to something greater, to find a glimmer of an answer to our half-formed questions.

Some of the people who seek spiritual solace in the wilderness are "believers" in the traditional sense; they are devout, practicing members of a mainstream religion. A wilderness retreat renews and intensifies their faith. Many others, however, are agnostics or atheists. In fact, such people are probably far more common in wilderness areas than they are in the general population. First of all, wilderness visitors are more likely than the average citizen to have an education beyond a bachelor's degree. Secondly, people with college degrees are more likely than others to consider themselves agnostics or atheists. These wilderness pilgrims are also likely to have at least a popular culture-based knowledge of ecology, a respectable science that—because of its emphasis on interdependence—easily becomes a means for agnostics and atheists to express their religious impulses.

Wilderness, then, has a spiritual connotation for both believers and non-believers in a personal God. Many people in both groups travel to wilderness areas to experience a kind of transcendence, a connection with something beyond themselves, something that brings more meaning to everyday life. Whether or not they feel comfortable with the word "God," these modern pilgrims share the same basic needs and seek the same basic experience.

This book is for all those who see a wilderness trip as *more* than a vacation, *more* than a chance to paddle or hike in a wild setting, *more* than a photo opportunity or a fishing expedition. The book was compiled for those who enjoy these things but seek something deeper—*re*-creation rather than mere recreation. Like a bound version of Sigurd Olson's medicine bag, *The Wilderness Companion* contains brief quotations that should encourage readers to reflect on their own search for meaning. It is not meant to be exhaustive, but merely a starting point for what is inherently a personal process. The quotations come from an eclectic group of people who, if you could gather them together, would disagree strongly with each other on matters of faith and theology, and yet surprisingly often would agree with each other's insights regarding the human condition. Perhaps this book will help break down barriers of religious prejudice that often prevent us from acknowledging the grains of truth in the words of those whose beliefs differ from ours.

The Wilderness Companion begins by looking at what others have said about the search for meaning; if nothing else, it helps us to remember that we are not alone, that the search is an essential element distinguishing humans from other animals. The next section reflects on the spiritual benefits we may receive by spending time in nature. Recognition of these benefits should, at the very least, make us think about how we in turn treat nature, and so the third section looks at the concept of stewardship.

From there we examine the key attributes of wilderness— silence and solitude, both of which are necessary for spiritual growth. Following them is a section called "Questions," which acts as a bridge to the rest of the book. Silence and solitude provide the environmental conditions we need in order to ask our hidden questions and to hear the silent answers; awareness and aliveness are the human prerequisites. Together, these elements help us discover beauty, mystery, and a sense of harmony and oneness, as the next four sections intimate.

We will also find hardship, both in our wilderness excursions and in our life journeys, and if we don't open ourselves to it we cannot go far in our search for meaning. We never will experience true joy if we close ourselves off from sorrow. The middle of the book, therefore, contains some serious and not-so-serious thoughts on adversity.

The largest part of the book is devoted to fruits of the search for meaning. Some of these, such as humility, detachment, and love, are not only fruits, but also are necessary for spiritual progress during the journey. Others are pure gift. We may learn to see time, evolution, and life itself with new eyes; we may come to better know ourselves; we may place knowledge and truth in a broader perspective; we may become open to that heightened combination of awareness and aliveness called contemplation, and possibly experience a sudden flash of insight, an epiphany. Some of us may feel the presence of God and be filled with a quiet but lasting joy.

I am deeply grateful to all those people whose inspiration and wisdom have touched me on my own journey. A number of them appear in the following pages, particularly Sigurd Olson and Thomas Merton. But many others, such as my family, friends, and gifted teachers, are not quoted in this book and yet are contributors just the same because they have become part of me. I would like to single out just two: Jim Egan and Tony McCarthy. More than they realize, they have been my spiritual guides. They have helped me see the boulders in my river of life, and have shown me the surest route to the distant, shining sea. If I still often manage to run into the rocks or lose my way, it is through no fault of theirs. They are trusty guides, and true wilderness companions.

—David Backes

❖ THE SEARCH ❖

Mostly the animals understand their roles, but man, by comparison, seems troubled by a message that, it is often said, he cannot quite remember, or has gotten wrong. Implied in this is our feeling that life demands an answer from us, that an essential part of man is his struggle to remember the meaning of the message with which he has been entrusted, that we are, in fact, message carriers. We are not what we seem. We have had a further instruction.
— *Loren Eiseley* —

Man is discontented with a single role. He wants to play all roles. Questing, unsatisfied, he is perennially the discontented animal . . . This restless quest has produced the field glasses through which I watch the hawk and the sparrow. It has produced the materials with which I set down these words. It has also produced the poisons that drench the land and flow down the rivers, the chemical pollution in the air, the abused forests, the extinct wildlife, the threat to man's survival on earth. What direction this questing, this eternal discontent, will take in the future is of concern to the hawk and to the sparrow—and to me.
— *Edwin Way Teale* —

My soul is like the oar that momently
  Dies in a desperate stress beneath the wave,
Then glitters out again and sweeps the sea:
  Each second I'm new-born from some new grave.
— *Sidney Lanier* —

I move, unseeing, toward an absolute
So bright within it darkens all I am;
Am dropped away: dropped out of time,
One still too frail to bear himself, alone . . .
  — Theodore Roethke —

I long ago lost a hound, a bay horse, and a turtle dove and am still
on their trail. Many are the travelers I have spoken to concerning
them, describing their tracks and to what calls they answered. I
have met one or two who have heard the hound and the tramp of
the horse, and even seen the dove disappear behind a cloud, and
they seemed as anxious to recover them as if they had lost them
themselves.
  — Henry David Thoreau —

What a long way the ancestral memory has to go, seeking, like a
pale sleuth-hound among obscure dusks and forgotten nocturnal
silences, for the lost trails of the soul.
  — Fiona Macleod —

Only great sorrow or great joy can reveal your truth.
If you would be revealed you must either dance naked in the sun, or
carry your cross.
  — Kahlil Gibran —

God had called us, and we came,
  But the blessed road I trod
Was a bitter road to me,
  And at heart I questioned God.
  — Edna St. Vincent Millay —

The world may be known
Without leaving the house;
The Way may be seen
Apart from the windows.
The further you go,
The less you will know.
Accordingly, the Wise Man
Knows without going,
Sees without seeing,
Does without doing.
— *Lao Tzu* —

There is also, of course, one's internal mapless country—what John
Muir biographer Michael Cohen calls the *pathless way*. Toward this I
navigate. It cannot be helped. It is the way of mind and spirit
leading to the most intriguing, most powerful landscape of all.
— *Jim dale Vickery* —

The Inner Light is beyond praise and blame;
Like space it knows no boundaries,
Yet it is ever here, within us, ever retaining its
    serenity and fulness.
It is only when you hunt for it that you lose it;
You cannot take hold of it, but equally you cannot get
    rid of it,
And while you can do neither, it goes on its own way.
You remain silent and it speaks; you speak, and it is
    dumb;
The great gate of charity is wide open, with no
    obstacles before it.
— *Yung-chia Ta-shih* —

You say there is no substance here,
    One great reality above:
Back from that void I shrink in fear,
    And child-like hide myself in love:
Show me what angels feel. Till then
I cling, a mere weak man, to men.
    — *William Cory* —

Patience, patience, patience is what the sea teaches. Patience and faith. One should lie empty, open, choiceless as a beach— waiting for a gift from the sea.
    — *Anne Morrow Lindbergh* —

If only we too could discover a pure, contained,
human place, our own strip of fruit-bearing soil
between river and rock. For our own heart always exceeds us . . .
And we can no longer follow it, gazing
into images that soothe it or into the godlike bodies
where, measured more greatly, it achieves a greater repose.
    — *Rainer Maria Rilke* —

Lo, yonder the holy place.
Swift and far I journey,
To life unending, and beyond it . . .
To joy unchanging, and beyond it.
Yea, swift and far I journey.
    — *Navajo song* —

I am being driven forward
Into an unknown land.
The pass grows steeper,
The air colder and sharper.
A wind from my unknown goal
Stirs the strings
Of expectation.

Still the question:
Shall I ever get there?
There where life resounds,
A clear pure note
In the silence.
    — *Dag Hammarskjöld* —

Give me my scallop shell of quiet,
My staff of faith to walk upon,
My scrip of joy, immortal diet,
My bottle of salvation,
My gown of glory, hope's true gage
And thus I'll take my pilgrimage.
    — *Sir Walter Raleigh* —

❖ NATURE'S SPIRITUAL VALUES ❖

Nature is a part of our humanity, and without some awareness and experience of that divine mystery man ceases to be man. When the Pleiades and the wind in the grass are no longer a part of the human spirit, a part of very flesh and bone, man becomes, as it were, a kind of cosmic outlaw, having neither the completeness and integrity of the animal nor the birthright of a true humanity.
— *Henry Beston* —

While seeking the secrets of nature I have watched the salutary effects of stillness and peace on human hearts and minds. I have seen the overpowering beauty of dawns and sunsets reach into troubled breasts and heal hurts that were thought beyond medicine and philosophy. And I have seen those burdened with grief take on the silence of the forest aisles until they could hear that still, small voice which lifts hope and faith with wordless assurance.
— *Sam Campbell* —

The spirit seems to inhabit no time and no space at all, but it thrashes and resounds when it meets the world, like a tuning fork which has been struck against the edge of a table. By its sudden music we know it is there.
— *Diana Kappel-Smith* —

There are yet many boys to be born who, like Isaiah, "may see, and know, and consider, and understand together, that the hand of the Lord hath done this." But where shall they see, and know, and consider? In museums?
— *Aldo Leopold* —

We take from nature what we cannot see.
— *Theodore Roethke* —

Wildness is a necessity. Mountain peaks and reservations are useful, not only as fountains of timber and irrigating rivers, but as Fountains of Life!
— *John Muir* —

Ah, drink again
This river that is the taker-away of pain,
And the giver-back of beauty! . . .
Immerse the dream.
Drench the kiss.
Dip the song in the stream.
— *Edna St. Vincent Millay* —

It's the beauty that thrills me with wonder,
It's the stillness that fills me with peace.
— *Robert Service* —

If we can only come back to nature together every year, and consider the flowers and the birds, and confess our faults and mistakes and our unbelief under these silent stars, and hear the river murmuring our absolution, we shall die young, even though we live long: we shall have a treasure of memories which will be like a twinflower, always a double blossom on a single stem, and carry with us into the unseen world something which will make it worth while to be immortal.
— *Henry Van Dyke* —

What, pray tell, would I buy? There is nothing out here that is not free for the asking. Can you buy a sunrise? Is there a price to the exhilaration we feel from the thunderstorm that rages outside? Nature is the truest democracy, and not the richest man in the world is served a grander sunset than the beggar.
— *Michael Furtman* —

What I know of the divine sciences and Holy Scripture, I learnt in woods and fields. I have had no other masters than the beeches and the oaks.

— *St. Bernard* —

From the cool cisterns of the midnight air
   My spirit drank repose;
The fountain of perpetual peace flows there,
   From those deep cisterns flows.
   — *Henry Wadsworth Longfellow* —

Forests are made for weary men,
That they might find their souls again;
And little leaves are hung on trees,
To whisper of old memories;
And trails with cedar shadows black,
Are placed there just to lead men back
Beyond the pitfalls of success,
To boyhood, peace and happiness.
   — *Mary Carolyn Davies* —

Oh, what is abroad in the marsh and the terminal sea?
Somehow my soul seems suddenly free
From the weighing of fate and the sad discussion of sin,
By the length and the breadth and the sweep of the marshes of
 Glynn.
   — *Sidney Lanier* —

❖ STEWARDSHIP ❖

All men are brothers, we like to say, half-wishing sometimes in secret it were not true. But perhaps it is true. And is the evolutionary line from protozoan to Spinoza any less certain? That also may be true. We are obliged, therefore, to spread the news, painful and bitter though it may be for some to hear, that all living things on earth are kindred.
— *Edwin Abbey* —

Unless we accept the evidence that we are but part of the complex whole, that each creature on earth is here to live its own life, without any more regard for man's wishes or his welfare than for the wishes and welfare of any other dweller on the planet, we are destined to live and die without being able to reconcile what seems to us *should be* with what *is*.
— *Edwin Way Teale* —

The last word in ignorance is the man who says of an animal or plant: "What good is it?" If the land mechanism as a whole is good, then every part is good, whether we understand it or not. If the biota, in the course of aeons, has built something we like but do not understand, then who but a fool would discard seemingly useless parts? To keep every cog and wheel is the first part of intelligent tinkering.
— *Aldo Leopold* —

The man who sat on the ground in his tipi meditating on life and its meaning, accepting the kinship of all creatures and acknowledging unity with the universe of things was infusing into his being the true essence of civilization.
— *Chief Luther Standing Bear* —

Man did not weave the web of life. He is merely a strand in it. Whatever he does to the web, he does to himself.
— *Chief Seattle* —

There is no scavenger that eats tin cans, and no wild thing leaves a like disfigurement on the forest floor.
— *Mary Austin* —

Now we stand in the bold afternoon of our days on earth. We straddle the oceans with legs of bronze, like the Colossus. Our shadow is long into space, for we dream to the stars. Nature will be forced to remember us, by the stripes we gave her, and the mark of the iron bracelet, by the way we stripped her, by the lives she gave for us and the children she bore to us, and the death we died in her arms, spoiled children, after all, children of her own.
— *Donald Culross Peattie* —

A thing is right when it tends to preserve the integrity, stability, and beauty of the biotic community. It is wrong when it tends otherwise.
— *Aldo Leopold* —

If a tree dies, plant another in its place.
— *Linnaeus* —

Without love of the land, conservation lacks meaning or purpose, for only in a deep and inherent feeling for the land can there be dedication in preserving it.
— *Sigurd F. Olson* —

All creatures have the same source as we have. Like us, they derive the life of thought, love, and will from the Creator. Not to hurt our humble brethren is our first duty to them; but to stop there is a complete misapprehension of the intentions of Providence. We have a higher mission. God wishes that we should succor them whenever they require it.
— *St. Francis of Assisi* —

Francis of Assisi's loving and contemplative reverence in the face of nature survives today in the awareness of man's kinship to all other living things and in the conservation movement. But reverence is not enough, because man has never been a passive witness of nature. He changes the environment by his very presence, and his only options in his dealings with the earth are to be destructive or constructive. To be creative, man must relate to nature with his senses as much as with his common sense, with his heart as much as with knowledge. He must read the book of external nature and the book of his own nature, to discern the common patterns and harmonies.

— *René Dubos* —

Hasidism has a tradition that one of man's purposes is to assist God in the work of redemption by "hallowing" the things of creation. By a tremendous heave of his spirit, the devout man frees the divine sparks trapped in the mute things of time; he uplifts the forms and moments of creation, bearing them aloft into that rare air and hallowing fire in which all clays must shatter and burst.

— *Annie Dillard* —

A human life, so often likened to a spectacle upon a stage, is more justly a ritual. The ancient values of dignity, beauty, and poetry which sustain it are of Nature's inspiration; they are born of the mystery and beauty of the world. Do no dishonour to the earth lest you dishonour the spirit of man. Hold your hands out over the earth as over a flame. To all who love her, who open to her the doors of their veins, she gives of her strength, sustaining them with her own measureless tremor of dark life. Touch the earth, love the earth, honour the earth, her plains, her valleys, her hills, and her seas; rest your spirit in her solitary places. For the gifts of life are the earth's and they are given to all, and they are the songs of birds at daybreak, Orion and the Bear, and dawn seen over ocean from the beach.

— *Henry Beston* —

Let us each build our own land ethic first, stone by stone as if in a wall, and we may find that this fence is substantially complete, our neighbors busy building, too, all the while we struggled.

— *Michael Furtman* —

❖ SILENCE ❖

The twentieth century is, among other things, the Age of Noise . . .
And this din goes far deeper, of course, than the ear-drums. It
penetrates the mind, filling it with a babel of distractions—news
items, mutually irrelevant bits of information, blasts of corybantic or
sentimental music, continually repeated doses of drama that bring
no catharsis, but merely create a craving for daily or even hourly
emotional enemas.
  — *Aldous Huxley* —

Silence is the element in which great things fashion themselves.
  — *Thomas Carlyle* —

And silence, like a poultice, comes
To heal the blows of sound.
  — *Oliver Wendell Holmes* —

Over all, rocks, wood, and water, brooded the spirit of repose, and
the silent energy of nature stirred the soul to its inmost depths.
  — *Thomas Cole* —

The birds are going, and their slight songs.
I am ready for a deeper silence.
  — *Theodore Roethke* —

The silence ground my soul keen like a spear.
  — *Sidney Lanier* —

I saw old Autumn in the misty morn
Stand shadowless like silence, listening
To silence.
— *Thomas Hood* —

I have lain and listened through the heavy calm of a tropical
voyage, hour after hour, longing for a sound; and in desert nights the
dead stillness has many a time wakened me from sleep. For
moments, too, in my forest life, the groves made absolutely no
breath of movement; but there is around these summits the
soundlessness of a vacuum. The sea stillness is that of sleep; the
desert, death—this silence is like the waveless calm of space.
— *Clarence King* —

And then there crept
A little noiseless noise among the leaves,
Born of the very sigh that silence heaves.
— *John Keats* —

At times on quiet waters one does not speak aloud but only in
whispers, for then all noise is sacrilege.
—*Sigurd F. Olson* —

What a silence! The river is roaring past like the river of time itself, but we have forgotten it, we have detached ourselves from it, and beside our little fire there is a silence all our own. We have a silence and a noise at the same time.

— Stephen Graham —

Let those who can stand a little silence find other people who like silence, and create silence and peace for one another.

— Thomas Merton —

Sixty-six times have these eyes beheld the changing
scenes of Autumn.
I have said enough about moonlight,
Ask me no more.
Only listen to the voice of pines and cedars, when no wind stirs.

— Ryo-Nen —

❖ SOLITUDE ❖

It is in solitude, in quiet communion with nature, that we reach most deeply into truth.
— *Sam Campbell* —

Solitude is a silent storm that breaks down all our
dead branches;
Yet it sends our living roots deeper into the
living heart of the living earth.
— *Kahlil Gibran* —

We seem so frightened today of being alone that we never let it happen. Even if family, friends, and movies should fail, there is still the radio or television to fill up the void.
— *Anne Morrow Lindbergh* —

Solitude may strike self-conscious man as an affliction, but his march is away from his origins, and even his art is increasingly abstract and self-centered. From the solitude of the wood he has passed to the more dreadful solitude of the heart.
— *Loren Eiseley* —

There perhaps are souls that never weary, that go always unhalting and glad, tuneful and songful as mountain water. Not so, weary, hungry me. In all God's mountain mansions, I find no human sympathy, and I hunger.

— *John Muir* —

Wherever one goes one has one's self for company.

— *Joseph Wood Krutch* —

The man who goes alone can start today; but he who travels with another must wait till that other is ready.

— *Henry David Thoreau* —

Each soul must meet the morning sun, the new sweet earth and the Great Silence alone!

— *Ohiyesa, Santee Dakota doctor* —

Into solitude went I
And wisdom was revealed to me.
— *From a Winnebago song* —

Those who love solitude have a special claim on Providence and must rely on God's love for them even more blindly than anyone else.
— *Thomas Merton* —

Wilderness can be appreciated only by contrast, and solitude understood only when we have been without it. We cannot separate ourselves from society, comradeship, sharing, and love. Unless we can contribute something from wilderness experience, derive some solace or peace to share with others, then the real purpose is defeated.
— *Sigurd F. Olson* —

❖ QUESTIONS ❖

What is the secret of the mysterious enjoyment felt here—the strange calm, the divine frenzy? Whence comes the annihilation of bonds that seemed everlasting?

— John Muir —

What if I fell in a forest: Would a tree hear?

— Annie Dillard —

Is it heedless?
Is it heartless, or unjudging, or forgetful, or immune?
Do we apprehend its nature, can we comprehend its power,
We, as mortal as the sparrow, and as fading as the flower,
And as changing as the Moon?

— John Masefield —

What do we know about seasons anyway?

— Robert Finch —

What is a thunderstorm, to a bird?
— *John Hay* —

What course after nightfall has destiny written
that we must run to the end?
— *Pindar* —

Does perhaps a balance stand
Between the Devil on one hand
And God on the other, which must be gained
As often as lost, and so maintained?—
And what I love as my own soul
I spit upon—to make me whole?
— *Edna St. Vincent Millay* —

Is your disgust at your emptiness to be the only life with which you fill it?
— *Dag Hammarskjöld* —

Why do I persist in *thinking* that behind a closed door
lies nothing at all?
— *Diana Kappel-Smith* —

Perhaps the most urgent and practical renunciation is the renunciation of all questions.
— *Thomas Merton* —

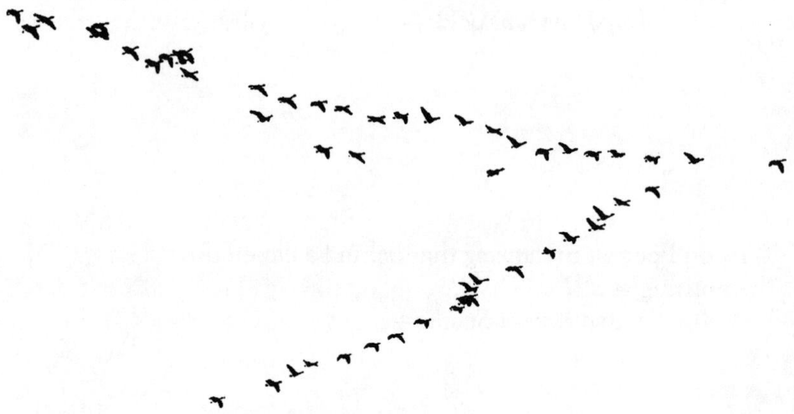

❖ AWARENESS ❖

Most people are *on* the world, not in it—have no conscious sympathy or relationship to anything about them—undiffused, separate, and rigidly alone like marbles of polished stone, touching but separate.
— *John Muir* —

As adults, we are preoccupied with living. As a consequence, we see little. At the approach of age some men look about them at last and discover the hole in the hedge leading to the unforeseen. By then, there is frequently no child companion to lead them safely through. After one or two experiences of getting impaled on thorns, the most persistent individual is apt to withdraw and to assert angrily that no such opening exists.
— *Loren Eiseley* —

If we had a keen vision of all that is ordinary in human life, it would be like hearing the grass grow or the squirrel's heart beat, and we should die of that roar which is the other side of silence.
— *George Eliot* —

If I knew all there is to know about a golden arctic poppy growing on a rocky ledge in the Far North, I would know the whole story of evolution and creation.
— *Sigurd F. Olson* —

We are laid asleep
In body, and become a living soul:
While with an eye made quiet by the power
Of harmony, and the deep power of joy,
We see into the life of things.
— *William Wordsworth* —

The whole secret of the study of nature lies in learning
how to use one's eyes.
— George Sand —

In nature, one never really sees a thing for the first time until one
has seen it for the fiftieth.
— Joseph Wood Krutch —

The eye may see for the hand, but not for the mind.
—Henry David Thoreau —

We see well at a distance; we see form, and color. But our nose has
one-sixtieth the power of a dog's nose. A bee can smell his mate two
miles away. A fly can see motion in all directions from hundreds of
spiraling lenses. A mosquito can assay the chemistries of water with
her hind leg to see if it is good for laying eggs in. A bat knows about
the jut of a twig and the flight of a moth by shouting into the void
and listening for echos. But . . . all of our focuses are narrowed; and
our myopic view is the only view—according to the great selecting
wisdoms of survival—that makes *sense*.
— Diana Kappel-Smith —

If you lie out flat on the stones—it seems odd to try, I know—you
will feel—here, that's it—the warmth of the sunlight emanating
from the stones. Turn your head to the side, ear to rock, and you will
hear the earth revolving on its axis and an adjustment of stones in
the riverbed. The heartbeats of salmon roe. One day I heard the
footsteps of someone miles away, following someone else.
— Barry Lopez —

That soul was there apparent, not revealed,
Unearthly meanings covered every tree.
— *John Masefield* —

Did you know that trees talk? Well they do. They talk to each other, and they'll talk to you if you listen . . . I have learned a lot from trees: sometimes about the weather, sometimes about animals, sometimes about the Great Spirit.
— *Tatanga Mani, a Stoney Indian* —

Like the wind, a brook exists only through motion. Down the narrow groove it has worn in the earth, hurrying toward the greater valleys of the rivers that will carry it to the sea, all the dark water foaming and gurgling below me rushes away into the night. The stream flows on and on. So the long life of the ever-renewing brook extends through the years. But it continues without awareness, without sensation, without emotion. Its existence is one of action, of music, of beauty; but it is life without life. The great gift of *our* lives is awareness.
— *Edwin Way Teale* —

❖ ALIVENESS ❖

Life demands participation. What we need is not kid gloves, in approved wrappings, but kids' eyes, sharp new eyes to pierce another layer of the mystery.
— *Robert Finch* —

Nature affects our minds as light affects the photographic emulsion on a film. Some films are more sensitive than others; some minds are more receptive.
— *Edwin Way Teale* —

I am alive to it, to the wind wherever it lists, however it makes itself manifest, like a movement of time itself among the vast spaces of the universes.
— *August Derleth* —

I could not sleep for thinking of the sky,
The unending sky, with all its million suns
Which turn their planets everlastingly
In nothing, where the fire-haired comet runs.
— *John Masefield* —

Sieze the day, put no trust in the morrow!
— *Horace* —

❖ BEAUTY ❖

Without a poignant consciousness of the goods of life, in all their freshness and intensity, without some daily glimpse of beauty, some expression of tenderness, some stir of passion, some release in gaiety and laughter, some quickening of rhythm and music, our very humanity is not safe.
— *Lewis Mumford* —

The experience of beauty is pure, self-manifest, compounded equally of joy and consciousness, free from admixture of any other perception, the very twin brother of mystical experience, and the very life of it is super-sensuous wonder.
— *Visvanatha* —

Never lose an opportunity of seeing anything that is beautiful; for beauty is God's handwriting—a wayside sacrament. Welcome it in every fair face, in every fair sky, in every fair flower, and thank God for it as a cup of blessing.
— *Ralph Waldo Emerson* —

Everybody needs beauty as well as bread, places to play in and pray in where Nature may heal and cheer and give strength to body and soul alike.
— *John Muir* —

Is not beauty created at every encounter between a man and life, in which he repays his debt by focusing on the living moment all the power which life has given him as an obligation? Beauty—for the one who pays his debt. For others, too, perhaps.
— *Dag Hammarskjöld* —

Beauty never stands alone, [and] is so fragile it can be destroyed by a sound or a foreign thought. It may be infinitesimally small or encompass the universe itself.
— *Sigurd F. Olson* —

Beauty is truth, truth beauty—that is all
Ye know on earth, and all ye need to know.
— *John Keats* —

Beauty is nothing
but the beginning of terror, which we still are just
        able to endure,
and we are so awed because it serenely disdains
to annihilate us.
— *Rainer Maria Rilke* —

When we look around us and marvel how nature has placed us in surroundings of beauty, making life more rich and pleasant, how can we be sure we are not using, as our own yardstick of beauty, merely the things with which we have become familiar? In some future time, in a world divorced from nature, will a brick instead of a flower, the whir of an electric fan instead of the song of a thrush, the straight line of a skyscraper instead of the curve of a winding brook be considered examples of the beautiful? We find our beauty in the things we know.
— *Edwin Way Teale* —

Great beauty captures me, but a beauty still greater frees me
even from itself.
— *Kahlil Gibran* —

How paint it; how describe? None has the power.
It only had the power upon the soul
To consecrate the spirit and the hour,
To light to sudden rapture and console,
Its beauty called a truce: forgave: forgot
All the long horror of man's earthly lot,
A miracle unspeakable of flower
In a green May unutterably blue.
— *John Masefield* —

After the feet of beauty fly my own.
— *Edna St. Vincent Millay* —

In beauty may I walk . . .
On the trail of pollen may I walk,
With dew about my feet may I walk,
In old age wandering on a trail of beauty,
Livingly, may I walk . . .
In beauty be it finished.
— *Navajo prayer* —

❖ MYSTERY ❖

Out there is a different world, older and greater and deeper by far than ours, a world which surrounds and sustains the little world of men as sea and sky surround and sustain a ship.
— *Edward Abbey* —

It comes along the ways of silence; along the ways of sound: its light feet are on sunrays and on shadows. Like dew, one knows not whether it is mysteriously gathered from below or secretly come from on high: simply it is there, above, around, beneath . . . Where the forest murmurs there is music: ancient, everlasting.
— *Fiona Macleod* —

The birth of dawn from sun and darkness is a mystery, very sacred, though it happens every day.
— *From a Pawnee song* —

This is the forest primeval. The murmuring pines and
the hemlocks,
Bearded with moss, and in garments green, indistinct in
the twilight,
Stand like Druids of eld, with voices sad and prophetic,
Stand like harpers hoar, with beards that rest on their
bosoms.
Loud from its rocky caverns, the deep-voiced neighboring ocean
Speaks, and in accents disconsolate answers the wail of the
forest.
— *Henry Wadsworth Longfellow* —

Listen to the voice of the wind
and the ceaseless message that forms itself out of
    silence.
    —Rainer Maria Rilke —

Wind woke my hair; a tune died on a stone.
The dark heart of some most ancient thing . . .
    — Theodore Roethke —

It was not any human voice, and yet it had a human ring. It was not the voice of any beast, and yet it came, as it were, from the strength of a beast. It could not be the voice of a bird, no bird could be big enough, and yet there was something birdlike in its tone. If it were not the voice of a man, beast or bird, what could it be? . . . It was not sorrowful nor joyful nor terrible. It was great and strange. It came from the heart of the wilderness or rock, miles from any human dwelling. It was like the rock speaking.
    — John Masefield —

There is an indefinable mysterious Power that pervades everything. I feel it, though I do not see it. It is this Unseen Power which makes itself felt and yet defies all proof, because it is so unlike all that I perceive through my senses. It transcends the senses.
— *Mahatma Gandhi* —

Talk of mysteries! Think of our life in nature—daily to be shown matter, to come in contact with it—rocks, trees, wind on our cheeks! the *solid* earth! the *actual* world! the *common sense*! *Contact! Contact! Who* are we? *where* are we?
— *Henry David Thoreau* —

❖ HARMONY ❖

[The] song of the waters is audible to every ear, but there is other music in these hills, by no means audible to all. To hear even a few notes of it you must first live here for a long time, and you must know the speech of hills and rivers. Then on a still night, when the campfire is low and the Pleiades have climbed over rimrocks, sit quietly and listen for a wolf to howl, and think hard of everything you have seen and tried to understand. Then you may hear it—a vast pulsing harmony—its score inscribed on a thousand hills, its notes the lives and deaths of plants and animals, its rhythms spanning the seconds and the centuries.

— *Aldo Leopold* —

All things work together:
I have watched them reverting,
And have seen how they flourish
And return again, each to his roots.
— *Lao Tzu* —

From above, to a hawk, the bend must appear only natural and I for the moment inseparably a part, like salmon or a flower. I cannot say well enough how this single perception has dismantled my loneliness.

— *Barry Lopez* —

Silent, inaudible, invisible flow. The very mountains flowing to the sea. The great heart of the hills sending its life down in streams. Mountains die that we may live.

— *John Muir* —

Take the least of things; take a blue-grass blade. Its cells tense with the waters and pressure of living, it captures light, thrusts into the rushing flume of radiation a silent mill wheel. So a leaf obeys a star, a star subserves a leaf.

— *Donald Culross Peattie* —

It is wonderful that the moon travels along the equator at the rate of a thousand miles an hour: but more wonderful that these loose, formless, blind and insensate waters should awake at the touch of that pale hand, should move to it and follow it as the flocks of the hills to the voice of the shepherd.

— *Fiona Macleod* —

Everything an Indian does is in a circle, because the power of the world always works in circles, and everything tries to be round . . . The sky is round, and the earth is round like a ball, and so are all the stars. The wind, in its greatest power, whirls. Birds make their nests in circles, for their religion is the same as ours. The sun comes forth and goes down again in a circle. The moon does the same, and both are round . . . Even the seasons form a great circle in their changing, and always come back again to where they were. The life of a man is a circle from childhood to childhood, and so it is in everything where power moves.

— *Black Elk* —

"The ruin or the blank that we see when we look at Nature," [Emerson] says, "is in our own eye." Is it not equally true that the harmony and perfection that we see are in our own eye also? In fact, are not all the qualities and attributes which we ascribe to Nature equally the creation of our own minds? The beauty, the sublimity, the power of Nature are experiences of the beholder. The drudge in the fields does not experience them, but the poet, the thinker, the seer, does . . . Nature is what we make her.

— *John Burroughs* —

❖ ONENESS ❖

We are not cut off, we are not isolated points; the great currents flow through us and over us and around us, and unite us to the whole of nature.
— *John Burroughs* —

We are part of the earth and it is part of us. The flowers are our sisters. The deer, the horse, the great eagle, these are our brothers. The rocky crests, the juices in the meadows, the body heat of the pony and the man—all belong to the same family. The shining water that moves in streams and rivers is not just water, but the blood of our ancestors.
— *Chief Seattle* —

Man is not himself only, not solely a variation of his racial type in the pattern of his immediate experience. He is all that he sees; all that flows to him from a thousand sources, half noted, or noted not at all except by some sense that lies too deep for naming. He is the land, the lift of its mountain lines, the reach of its valleys; his is the rhythm of its seasonal processions, the involution and variation of its vegetal patterns. If there is in the country of his abiding, no more than a single refluent color . . . he takes it in and gives it forth again in directions and occasions least suspected by himself, as a manner, as music, as a prevailing tone of thought, as the line of his roof-tree, the pattern of his personal adornment.
— *Mary Austin* —

To stick your hands into the river is to feel the cords that bind the earth together in one piece.
— *Barry Lopez* —

All the water that has ever been or ever will be is here now. It sits, it runs, it rises as mist. It evaporates and falls again as rain or snow . . . You cannot pollute a drop of water anywhere without eventually poisoning some distant place.
— *Michael Furtman* —

Everything in Nature contains all the powers of Nature. Everything is made of one hidden stuff.
— *Ralph Waldo Emerson* —

Yea, I am one with all I see,
With wind and wave, with pine and palm;
Their very elements in me
Are fused to make me what I am.
Through me their common life-stream flows,
And when I yield this human breath,
In leaf and blossom, bud and rose,
Live on I will . . . There is no Death.
— *Robert Service* —

I dream of a hard and brutal mysticism in which the naked self merges with a non-human world and yet somehow survives still intact, individual, separate. Paradox and bedrock.
— *Edward Abbey* —

One Nature, perfect and pervading, circulates in all natures,
One Reality, all-comprehensive, contains within itself all
      realities.
The one Moon reflects itself wherever there is a sheet of water,
And all the moons in the waters are embraced within the one
      Moon.
The Dharma-body [the Absolute] of all the Buddhas enters into my
      own being.
And my own being is found in union with theirs.
— *Yung-chia Ta-shih* —

When is a man in mere understanding? I answer, "When a man sees one thing separated from another." And when is a man above mere understanding? That I can tell you: "When a man sees All in all, then a man stands beyond mere understanding."
— *Meister Eckhart* —

Learn to look with an equal eye upon all beings, seeing the one Self in all.
— *Srimad Bhagavatam* —

Talk as much philosophy as you please, worship as many gods as you like, observe all ceremonies, sing devoted praises to any number of divine beings—liberation never comes, even at the end of a hundred aeons, without the realization of the Oneness of Self.
— *Shankara* —

The extrahuman [lies] in the experience of the greatness of Nature. This does not allow itself to be reduced to an expression of our human reactions, nor can we share in it by expressing them. Unless we each find a way to chime in as one note in the organic whole, we shall only observe ourselves observing the interplay of its thousand components in a harmony outside our experience of it as harmony.
— *Dag Hammarskjöld* —

The air is in the sunshine and the sunshine in the air. So likewise is God in the being of the soul; and whenever the soul's highest powers are turned inward with active love, they are united with God without means, in a simple knowledge of all truth, and in an essential feeling and tasting of all good.
— *Jan Van Ruysbroeck* —

All are but parts of one stupendous whole,
Whose body Nature is, and God the soul.
— *Alexander Pope* —

The uniformity of the earth's life, more astonishing than its diversity, is accountable by the high probability that we derived, originally, from some single cell, fertilized in a bolt of lightning as the earth cooled. It is from the progeny of this parent cell that we take our looks; we still share genes around, and the resemblance of the enzymes of grasses to those of whales is a family resemblance.

— *Lewis Thomas* —

It was but yesterday I thought myself a fragment quivering without rhythm in the sphere of life.

Now I know that I am the sphere, and all life in rhythmic fragments moves within me.

— *Kahlil Gibran* —

Paradoxically, it is in such broad, spacious settings as this—raking the flats, handlining on the banks, working by himself in some common field of endeavor—that a man may feel least alone. The more he allies himself to some varied and interdependent whole, the less he is subject to sudden and wholesale bereavement by chance. His heart rests at the bottom of things; anchored there, he may cast about and never be at sea.

— *Robert Finch* —

❖ ADVERSITY ❖

My fingers were stiff and red with cold, and my nose ran. I had forgotten the Law of the Wild, which is, "Carry Kleenex."
— *Annie Dillard* —

Adversity is the state in which a man most easily becomes acquainted with himself, being especially free from admirers then.
— *Samuel Johnson* —

All bushes can't be bears.
— *Theodore Roethke* —

How we squander our hours of pain.
How we gaze beyond them into the bitter duration
to see if they have an end. Though they are really
our winter-enduring foliage, our dark evergreen,
one season in our inner year, not only a season
in time—but are place and settlement,
foundation and soil and home.
— *Rainer Maria Rilke* —

Mishaps are like knives, that either serve us or cut us, as we grasp them by the blade or the handle.
— *James Russell Lowell* —

Persons who have really suffered at the hands of others do not find it difficult to forgive, nor even to understand the people who caused their suffering. They do not find it difficult to forgive because out of suffering and sorrow truly endured comes an instinctive sense of privilege. Recognition of the creative truth comes in a flash: forgiveness for others, as for ourselves, for we too know not what we do.

— *Laurens Van der Post* —

And there is a Catskill eagle in some souls that can alike dive down into the blackest gorges, and soar out of them again and become invisible in the sunny spaces.

— *Herman Melville* —

The best way not to find the bed too cold is to go to bed colder than the bed is.

— *St. Charles Borromeo* —

Call on God, but row away from the rocks.

— *Indian proverb* —

While the fates permit, live happily; life spreads on with hurried step, and with winged days the wheel of the headlong year is turned.
— *Lucius Annaeus Seneca* —

Be happy while y'er leevin,
For y'er a lang time deid.
— *Scottish proverb* —

❖ HUMILITY ❖

It seems to me that humility is truth.
— *St. Therese of Lisieux* —

If you were to ask me what are the ways of God, I would tell you that the first is humility, the second is humility, and the third is still humility. Not that there are no other precepts to give, but if humility does not precede all that we do, our efforts are fruitless.
— *St. Augustine of Hippo* —

Then, some night, one stands solitary in the darkness, and feels less than the shadow of a leaf that has passed upon the wind . . .
— *Fiona Macleod* —

There is no star so startling as a morning planet. For it reminds us that other worlds than ours do not keep our hours nor move upon the rounds appointed to us.
— *Donald Culross Peattie* —

Would you become a pilgrim on the road of Love? The first condition is that you make yourself humble as dust and ashes.
— *Ansari of Herat* —

I knew nothing; I was nothing. For this reason God picked me out.
— *St. Catherine Laboure* —

Without humility, all will be lost.
— *St. Teresa of Avila* —

A man is humble when he stands in the truth with a knowledge and appreciation for himself as he really is.
— *The Cloud of Unknowing* —

Once the noble Ibrahim, as he sat on his throne,
Heard a clamor and noise of cries on the roof,
Also heavy footsteps on the roof of his palace.
He said to himself, "Whose heavy feet are these?"
He shouted from the window, "Who goes there?"
The guards, filled with confusion, bowed their heads,
      saying,
"It is we, going the rounds in search."
He said, "What seek ye?" They said, "Our camels."
He said, "Who ever searched for camels on a housetop?"
They said, "We follow thy example,
Who seekest union with God, while sitting on a throne."
— *Jalal al-Din Rumi* —

Nothing is weaker than water,
But when it attacks something hard
Or resistant, then nothing withstands it,
And nothing will alter its way . . .
Because of this the Wise Man says
That only one who bears the nation's shame
Is fit to be its hallowed lord;
That only one who takes upon himself
The evils of the world may be its king.
— *Lao Tzu* —

A good case can be made for our nonexistence as entities. We are not made up, as we had always supposed, of successively enriched packets of our own parts. We are shared, rented, occupied. At the interior of our cells, driving them, providing the oxidative energy that sends us out for the improvement of each shining day, are the mitochondria, and in a strict sense they are not ours. They turn out to be little separate creatures, the colonial posterity of migrant prokaryocytes, probably primitive bacteria that swam into ancestral precursors of our eukaryotic cells and stayed there. Ever since, they have maintained themselves and their ways, replicating in their own fashion, privately, with their own DNA and RNA quite different from ours. They are as much symbionts as the rhizobial bacteria in the roots of beans. Without them, we would not move a muscle, drum a finger, think a thought.
— *Lewis Thomas* —

❖ DETACHMENT ❖

We Americans are great on fillers, as if what we have, what we are, is not enough. We have a cultural tendency toward denial, but, being affluent, we strangle ourselves with what we can buy. We have only to look at the houses we build to see how we build *against* space, the way we drink against pain and loneliness. We fill up space as if it were a pie shell, with things whose opacity further obstructs our ability to see what is already there.

— *Gretel Ehrlich* —

Go free as the wind, living as true to Nature as those gray and buff people of the sequoias and the pines.

— *John Muir* —

A man is rich in proportion to the number of things which he can afford to let alone.

— *Henry David Thoreau* —

All that hunting—for what? A new horror.
Weep out my wants until my eyes are stone.
— *Theodore Roethke* —

To seek happiness is not to live happily. Perhaps it is more true to say that one finds happiness by not seeking it. The wisdom that teaches us deliberately to restrain our desire for happiness enables us to discover that we are already happy without realizing the fact.
— *Thomas Merton* —

The soul that is attached to anything, however much good there may be in it, will not arrive at the liberty of divine union. For whether it will be a strong wire rope or a slender and delicate thread that holds the bird, it matters not, if it really holds it fast; for, until the cord be broken, the bird cannot fly. So the soul, held by the bonds of human affections, however slight they may be, cannot, while they last, make its way to God.
— *St. John of the Cross* —

My body is like a drifting cloud—I ask for nothing, I want nothing.
— *Kamo no Chomei* —

Cease willfully to hear or see, and let yourselves feel the mystery of the twilight hour.
— *Sam Campbell* —

The secret waits for the insight
Of eyes unclouded by longing;
Those who are bound by desire
See only the outward container.
— *Lao Tzu* —

❖ LOVE ❖

There is no creation, in the end, except in the mood of love; and if we are impotent to love, the mere recounting of our sins will leave ashes in our mouths and cinders in our eyes.
— *Lewis Mumford* —

The soul lives by that which it loves rather than in the body which it animates. For it has not its life in the body, but rather gives it to the body and lives in that which it loves.
— *St. John of the Cross* —

Our present economic, social and international arrangements are based, in large measure, upon organized lovelessness. We begin by lacking charity towards Nature, so that instead of trying to co-operate with Tao or the Logos on the inanimate and subhuman levels, we try to dominate and exploit, we waste the earth's mineral resources, ruin its soil, ravage its forests, pour filth into its rivers and poisonous fumes into its air.
— *Aldous Huxley* —

Love flowers best in openness and freedom.
— *Edward Abbey* —

Our love is not misplaced here on earth . . . our sense of wonder and beauty is locked at the very deepest levels into the knotted reality and texture of the physical world from which we wrest a daily living.
— *Robert Finch* —

It is good to love the unknown.
— *Charles Lamb* —

The important thing is not to think much but to love much; and so do that which best stirs you to love.
— *St. Teresa of Avila* —

Perhaps it is always the destined role of the compassionate to be strangers among men. To fail and pass, to fail and come again . . . "Love makyth the lover and the living matters not," an old phrase came hesitantly to my lips. We would win, I thought steadily, if not in human guise then in another, for love was something that life in its infinite prodigality could afford. It was the failures who had always won, but by the time they won they had come to be called successes. This is the final paradox, which men call evolution.
— *Loren Eiseley* —

And we are put on earth a little space,
That we may learn to bear the beams of love,
And these black bodies and this sunburnt face
Is but a cloud, and like a shady grove.
— *William Blake* —

❖ TIME ❖

We are preoccupied with time. If we could learn to love space as deeply as we are now obsessed with time, we might discover a new meaning in the phrase to *live like men*.
— *Edward Abbey* —

The rush and pressure of modern life are a form, perhaps the most common form, of its innate violence. To allow oneself to be carried away by a multitude of conflicting concerns, to surrender to too many demands, to commit oneself to too many projects, to want to help everyone in everything is to succumb to violence. More than that, it is cooperation in violence. The frenzy of the activist . . . destroys his own inner capacity for peace. It destroys the fruitfulness of his own work, because it kills the root of inner wisdom which makes work fruitful.
— *Thomas Merton* —

When one finally arrives at the point where schedules are forgotten, and becomes immersed in ancient rhythms, one begins to live.
— *Sigurd F. Olson* —

The bush pilot asked an Indian how long it took him to reach his trapping cabin by canoe.

"Four days," was the Indian's reply.

The pilot told the Indian it would take only an hour by pontoon plane.

"Why?" remarked the Indian.

Our infatuation with speed and getting to a destination quickly often forces us to bypass many of life's most valuable and profound experiences.
— *Calvin Rutstrum* —

My today is more than today,
And I look with a hunter's eye
Toward eternity.
      — *Theodore Roethke* —

The present moment is significant, not as the bridge between past and future, but by reason of its contents, contents which can fill our emptiness and become ours, if we are capable of receiving them.
      — *Dag Hammarskjöld* —

Learn the pace of the universe which is ever constant, and seek not to race ahead or yet to drag behind. A new day has been added to your experience. It is not past nor is it lost, but is now yours forever. Beyond this lovely night comes another morning, another noon, and yet another night. It will always be so. Therefore, set your stride for eternity; abandon your will in favor of the universal order of things; and know only one duty: to look in wonderment at the endless unfoldment of infinite creation.
      — *Sam Campbell* —

A thousand miles an hour, day flies the Atlantic. It finds the tossing lightship, and picks up the white signal numbers on its gray flanks. It gives back to lonely driftwood, prophetic of land, and to sargassos of red kelp floating lazy and succulent, their existent shapes. It eats out darkness, leaving only the etched lines of the spars and masts of the fishing fleet. Meeting shore, it runs a finger of cold shine down marginal sand.
      — *Donald Culross Peattie* —

Only the mountain has lived long enough to listen objectively to the howl of a wolf.
— *Aldo Leopold* —

There is not a vast and lonely mountain that has not a fallen comrade among the low undulating ridges of the continual lowland; not one of these that has not in turn to feed the white dust of the plain or the sea-gathered sand of ancient or as yet unformed shores. For the hills pass, even as we, or the green leaf becomes sere, or the fruit that ripens to its fall; though we speak of them as everlasting, and find the subtlest spell of their incalculable charm in the overwhelming sense of their imagined eternity.
— *Fiona Macleod* —

Perhap's time's definition of coal is the diamond.
— *Kahlil Gibran* —

The created world is but a small parenthesis in eternity.
— *Sir Thomas Browne* —

The measure of life is a flame in the soul:
It is neither swift nor slow.
But the vision of time is the shadow cast
By the fleeting world on the body's wall;
When it fades there is neither future nor past,
But love is all in all.
— *Henry Van Dyke* —

❖ EVOLUTION ❖

Nothing—not mountains nor sea nor shore nor rocks—is *exactly* the same on two successive days. The changes may be imperceptible to us but they are there. Lichens are working on granite. Death is replacing life. Leaves are expanding and leaves are wilting. The world is never finished. Everything is going up or going down around us. The things we see most often, the species that are endlessly repeated in individuals, are the successes, the end product of unceasing evolution.

— *Edwin Way Teale* —

It is as if all that had been created were a single organism, simple as the one word yes—and then through constant trial and error, through the adding of single letters, a phrase or two, here a line, there another line transposed, all of them chance happenings and chaotic inspirations and all of them subject to the hard editings of survival—one had finished up with the *Encyclopedia Britannica*. No—a million encyclopedias! . . . But underneath the almost infinite variety of the complex live beings that are the result of all this, one can still touch that original assumption: the yes.

— *Diana Kappel-Smith* —

Nature is a great traveler, but she never gets away from home; she takes all her possessions along with her, and her course is without direction, and without beginning or end. The most startling contradiction you can make expresses her best. She is the sum of all opposites, the success of all failures, the good of all evil.

— *John Burroughs* —

Out of the hells of the sun, the needful and terrible emptiness of the spaces, comes all we know—the infinite individuality of every leaf in the wood, the holy beauty of the thrush's song, the sensitive ear of the listener.
— *Donald Culross Peattie* —

Man with all his noble qualities . . . with his godlike intellect which has penetrated into the movements and constitution of the solar system . . . still bears in his bodily frame the indelible stamp of his lowly origin.
— *Charles Darwin* —

It is ironic that the one thing that all religions recognize as separating us from our creator—our very self-consciousness—is also the one thing that divides us from our fellow creatures. It was a bitter birthday present from evolution, cutting us off at both ends.
— *Annie Dillard* —

We patronize [animals] for their incompleteness, for their tragic fate of having taken form so far below ourselves. And therein we err, and greatly err. For the animal shall not be measured by man. In a world older and more complete than ours they move finished and complete, gifted with extensions of the senses we have lost or never attained, living by voices we shall never hear. They are not brethren, they are not underlings, they are other nations, caught with ourselves in the net of life and time, fellow prisoners of the splendour and travail of the earth.
— *Henry Beston* —

Those of us who would rather not deny and renounce the richness of our own experience by thinking of it merely as some process of mechanical adaptation had better not get in the habit of seeing nothing but mechanism in the life histories of other living things.
— *Joseph Wood Krutch* —

In three billion years of slow change and groping effort only one living creature has succeeded in escaping the trap of specialization that has led in time to so much death and wasted endeavor. It is man, but the word should be uttered softly, for his story is not yet done.

— *Loren Eiseley* —

Evolution continues in our time, no longer on the physiological or anatomical plane but on the spiritual and moral plane. We are at the dawn of a new phase of evolution and the violent eddies due to this change in the order of things still conceal that fact from the eyes of the majority. The transition from the ancestral animal, still squirming within us, to Man is too recent for us to be able to understand the ensuing conflicts which often seem disconcerting and incomprehensible.

— *Pierre Lecomte du Noüy* —

What needs stressing, however, is that, from the angle of evolutionary humanism, the flowering of the individual is seen as having intrinsic value, as being an end in itself. In the satisfying exercise of our faculties, in the pure enjoyment of our experience, the cosmic process of evolution is bringing some of its possibilities to fruition. In individual acts of comprehension or love, in the enjoyment of beauty, in the inner experiences of peace and assurance, in the satisfactions of creative achievement, however humble, we are helping to realise human destiny.

— *Julian Huxley* —

❖ LIFE ❖

Our life is a faint tracing on the surface of mystery, like the idle, curved tunnels of leaf miners on the face of a leaf. We must somehow take a wider view, look at the whole landscape, really see it, and describe what's going on here. Then we can at least wail the right question into the swaddling band of darkness, or, if it comes to that, choir the proper praise.
— *Annie Dillard* —

I have seen a tree root burst a rock face on a mountain or slowly wrench aside the gateway of a forgotten city. This is a very cunning feat, which men take too readily for granted. Life, unlike the inanimate, will take the long way round to circumvent barrenness. A kind of desperate will resides even in a root.
— *Loren Eiseley* —

What is life? It is the flash of a firefly in the night. It is the breath of a buffalo in the wintertime. It is the little shadow which runs across the grass and loses itself in the sunset.
— *Crowfoot* —

Life can only be understood backwards; but it must be lived forwards.
— *Sören Kierkegaard* —

> My life is like the crane who cries a few times
> under the pine tree
> And like the silent light from the lamp
> in the bamboo grove.
> — *Po Chu-i* —

> My life is like a stroll upon the beach,
> As near the ocean's edge as I can go.
> — *Henry David Thoreau* —

Stop and consider! Life is but a day;
A fragile dewdrop on its perilous way
From a tree's summit; a poor Indian's sleep
While his boat hastens to the monstrous steep
Of Montmorenci.
— John Keats —

Often men are as little noticed between the hours of arrival and
departure as the martins high aloft in the summer morning sky.
— August Derleth —

Wherever there is life there is also unconscious absurdity and, at
least on man's level, conscious comedy.
— Joseph Wood Krutch —

I am sure one cannot love life enough; but I believe, too, one
mustn't confuse love of life with the love of certain things in it. One
cannot pick the moment and place as one pleases and say, "Enough!
This is all I want. This is how it is henceforth to be." That sort of
present betrays past and future. Life is its own journey; presupposes
its own change and movement, and one tries to arrest them at one's
eternal peril.
— Laurens Van der Post —

The earth . . . is a gem of rare and magic beauty hung in a trackless
space filled with lethal radiations and accompanied in its journey by
sister planets which are either viciously hot or dreadfully cold, arid,
and lifeless chunks of raw rock. Earth is choice, precious, and sacred
beyond all comparison or measure.
— William Pollard —

The sky is everlasting
And the earth is very old.
Why so? Because the world
Exists not for itself;
It can and will live on.
— Lao Tzu —

Not a cloud-memory in the sky. Not a ripple-memory on the lake, as if so complete in immortality that the very lake pulse were no longer needed, as if only the spiritual part of landscape life were left. I spring to my feet crying: "Heavens and earth! Rock is not light, not heavy, not transparent, not opaque, but every pore gushes, glows like a thought with immortal life!"

— *John Muir* —

We cannot but be struck by the disproportion between the duration of a man's life and the duration of his influence on future generations. Every one of us leaves a trail either modest or brilliant, and this conviction should make itself felt in all the acts of our lives . . . Every man can, if he wishes, leave a more or less brilliant trace behind him.

— *Pierre Lecomte du Noüy* —

O trees of life, when does your winter come?
We are not in harmony, our blood does not forewarn us
like migratory birds'. Late, overtaken,
we force ourselves abruptly onto the wind
and fall to earth at some iced-over lake.
Flowering and fading come to us both at once.

— *Rainer Maria Rilke* —

The blazing evidence of immortality is our dissatisfaction with any other solution.

— *Ralph Waldo Emerson* —

There is comfort in the thought that if there is no immortality, we shall not know it.

— *John Burroughs* —

And, at the last, a tree gives up its life to make for him a home, and a stone is stood on end for him. The last? No, of course, that is not the last of the story. The uneasy earth mound erodes away, in the end. The boards are punkwood and foxfire. With a slow tug of gravity, and a frost heave, earth claims back even her stone, rubs away the graving on it, tilts it, floors it, and finally scrawls her own idea of an epitaph, in lichen runes.

— *Donald Culross Peattie* —

❖ SELF-KNOWLEDGE ❖

Most people do not like themselves at all. They distrust themselves, put on masks and pomposities. They quarrel and boast and pretend and are jealous because they do not like themselves. But mostly they do not even know themselves well enough to form a true liking. They cannot see themselves well enough to form a true liking, and since we automatically fear and dislike strangers, we fear and dislike our stranger-selves.
— *John Steinbeck* —

A man has many skins in himself, covering the depths of his heart. Man knows so many things; he does not know himself. Why, thirty or forty skins or hides, just like an ox's or a bear's, so thick and hard, cover the soul. Go into your own ground and learn to know yourself there.
— *Meister Eckhart* —

Every man contains within himself a ghost continent—a place circled as warily as Antarctica was circled two hundred years ago by Captain James Cook.
— *Loren Eiseley* —

Which of my winds will take
The downdrift of myself?
My help's not in me.
These ashes sift themselves.
— *Theodore Roethke* —

In other living creatures ignorance of self is nature; in man it is vice.
— *Boethius* —

It is wisdom to know others;
It is enlightenment to know one's self.
— *Lao Tzu* —

I do believe the most of me
Floats under water; and men see
Above the wave a jagged small
Mountain of ice, and that is all.
Only the depths of other peaks
May know my substance when it speaks,
And steadfast through the grinding jam
Remain aware of what I am.
Myself, I think, shall never know
How far beneath the wave I go.
— *Edna St. Vincent Millay* —

A traveler am I and a navigator, and every day I discover a new region within my soul.
— *Kahlil Gibran* —

Any spot is a port of entry if we will only accept it for what it is, asking of me only that I bear witness and recognize myself for what I so manifestly am: a part of what I behold.
— *Robert Finch* —

Bird and man, each in his cycle, obeys his own dark laws.
— *August Derleth* —

Not to have known—as most men have not—either the mountain or the desert is not to have known one's self. Not to have known one's self is to have known no one, and to have known no one makes it relatively easy to suppose, as sociology commonly does, that the central problems are the problems of technology and politics.
— *Joseph Wood Krutch* —

Men go abroad to wonder at the height of mountains, at the huge waves of the sea, at the long courses of the rivers, at the vast compass of the ocean, at the circular motion of the stars, and they pass by themselves without wondering.
— *St. Augustine of Hippo* —

When one is a stranger to oneself then one is estranged from others too. If one is out of touch with oneself, then one cannot touch others.
— *Anne Morrow Lindbergh* —

One who is obsessed with his own inner unity is failing to face his disunion with God and with other men. For it is in union with others that our own inner unity is naturally and easily established. To be preoccupied with achieving inner unity first and then going on to love others is to follow a logic of disruption which is contrary to life.
— *Thomas Merton* —

If you dwelt in self-knowledge alone, you would despair; if you dwelt in the knowledge of God alone, you would be tempted to presumption. One must go with the other, and thus you will reach perfection.
— *St. Catherine of Siena* —

The road to self-knowledge does not pass through faith. But only through the self-knowledge we gain by pursuing the fleeting light in the depth of our being do we reach the point where we can grasp what faith is.
— *Dag Hammarskjöld* —

As the light grows, we see ourselves to be worse than we thought. We are amazed at our former blindness as we see issuing from our heart a whole swarm of shameful feelings, like filthy reptiles crawling from a hidden cave. But we must be neither amazed nor disturbed. We are not worse than we were; on the contrary, we are better. But while our faults diminish, the light we see them by waxes brighter, and we are filled with horror. So long as there is no sign of cure, we are unaware of the depth of our disease; we are in a state of blind presumption and hardness, the prey of self-delusion. While we go with the stream, we are unconscious of its rapid course; but when we begin to stem it ever so little, it makes itself felt.
— *Francois de Salignac de la Mothe Fénelon* —

❖ KNOWLEDGE ❖

What every man knows about himself and his world is but the most infinitesimal part of knowledge, and what he can know about someone else and someone else's world is even less than that.
— *August Derleth* —

There is a way of knowing which is at once underneath and above consciousness of knowing. There is a way in which the collective knowledge of mankind expresses itself, for the finite individual, through mere daily living: a way in which life itself is sheer knowing.
— *Laurens Van der Post* —

Dignity and beauty and meaning are given to our lives when we see far enough and wide enough, when we see the forces that minister to us, and the natural order of which we form a part.
— *John Burroughs* —

The frontiers are not east or west, north or south, but wherever a man fronts a fact.
— *Henry David Thoreau* —

You must not know too much, or be too precise or scientific about birds and trees and flowers and watercraft; a certain free margin, and even vagueness—perhaps ignorance, credulity—helps your enjoyment of these things.
— *Walt Whitman* —

No matter how far science has gone and will go in its exploration of the universe and of life and its processes, there are certain things it cannot do. One is to bring understanding and peace to a confused and troubled soul.
— *Sigurd F. Olson* —

A mathematical mysticism, even if it is indisputable, will never touch the heart of the people, no more than the chemical analysis of a painting can evoke the esthetic impression it produces. There exists a chasm between the world of quality and that of quantity which science can never bridge.
— *Pierre Lecomte du Noüy* —

❖ TRUTH ❖

As the least drop of wine tinges the whole goblet, so the least particle of truth colors our whole life. It is never isolated, or simply added as treasure to our stock. When any real progress is made, we unlearn and learn anew what we thought we knew before.
— *Henry David Thoreau* —

We are all convinced that we desire the truth above all . . . But actually, what we desire is not "the truth" so much as "to be in the right" . . . What we seek is not the pure truth, but the partial truth that justifies our prejudices, our limitations, our selfishness.
— *Thomas Merton* —

One of the most pathetic things about us human beings is our touching belief that there are times when the truth is not good enough for us; that it can and must be improved upon . . . It is the very truth we deny which so tenderly and forgivingly picks up the fragments and puts them together again.
— *Laurens Van der Post* —

One of the penalties of an ecological education is that one lives alone in a world of wounds. Much of the damage inflicted on land is quite invisible to laymen. An ecologist must either harden his shell and make believe that the consequences of science are none of his business, or he must be the doctor who sees the marks of death in a community that believes itself well and does not want to be told otherwise.

— *Aldo Leopold* —

I want to be able to look at and into a juniper tree, a piece of quartz, a vulture, a spider, and see it as it is in itself, devoid of all humanly ascribed qualities, anti-Kantian, even the categories of scientific description. To meet God or Medusa face to face, even if it means risking everything human in myself.

— *Edward Abbey* —

What I am after is less to meet God face to face than really to take in a beetle, a frog, or a mountain when I meet one.

— *Joseph Wood Krutch* —

He who listens to truth is not less than he who utters truth.
— *Kahlil Gibran* —

Wind over lake: the image of inner truth.
— *I Ching* —

To see a World in a grain of sand,
       And a Heaven in a wild flower,
Hold Infinity in the palm of your hand,
       And Eternity in an hour.
— *William Blake* —

❖ CONTEMPLATION ❖

When we start at the center of ourselves, we discover something worthwhile extending toward the periphery of the circle. We find again some of the joy in the now, some of the peace in the here, some of the love in me and thee which go to make up the kingdom of heaven and earth.
— *Anne Morrow Lindbergh* —

Whoever studies to reach contemplation should begin by searchingly enquiring of himself how much he loves. For love is the motive power of the mind, which draws it out of the world and raises it on high.
— *St. Gregory the Great* —

Unplanned contemplation comes softly as falling mist, or the first snows of autumn.
— *Sigurd F. Olson* —

How shall I grasp it? Do not grasp it. That which remains when there is no more grasping is the Self.
— *Panchadasi* —

Whenever, in the course of the daily hunt the red hunter comes upon a scene that is strikingly sublime—a black thundercloud with the rainbow's glowing arch above the mountain, a white waterfall in the heart of a green gorge; a vast prairie tinged with the blood-red of sunset—he pauses for an instant in the attitude of worship. He sees no need for setting apart one day in seven as a holy day, since to him all days are God's.

— *Ohiyesa, Santee Dakota doctor* —

The secret of seeing is to sail on solar wind. Hone and spread your spirit till you yourself are a sail, whetted, translucent, broadside to the merest puff.

— *Annie Dillard* —

Let us pause for a moment and listen. Voices of the ages are speaking. Hear the chorus of frogs, singing a song which was heard when the world was young, which smote the ears of dinosaur and flying reptile. Hear the monotone of insects and the rustle of aspen leaves stirred to dancing by the slightest breeze. Note the mystery of the night bird's call and catch the feel of measureless, dark distance stretching forth from you in every direction. Drink it in, until it becomes a part of you and you a part of it. Let no fragment of the universe escape—take the very stars in your love.

— *Sam Campbell* —

If the heart wanders or is distracted, bring it back to the point quite gently and replace it tenderly in its Master's presence. And even if you did nothing during the whole of your hour but bring your heart back and place it again in Our Lord's presence, though it went away every time you brought it back, your hour would be very well employed.

— *St. Francis de Sales* —

There are few contemplatives, because few souls are perfectly humble.
— *Thomas á Kempis* —

The fly that touches honey cannot use its wings; so the soul that clings to spiritual sweetness ruins its freedom and hinders contemplation.
— *St. John of the Cross* —

Perhaps what some people really mean by spirituality is "spiritual desire"—and that is a worse error than action driven by desire: the awful illusion of a supposed "contemplation" that is nothing but mute desire feeding on itself!
— *Thomas Merton* —

Touch ultimate emptiness,
Hold steady and still.
— *Lao Tzu* —

❖ EPIPHANY ❖

The awakened person seeks to live so that any day might be good enough to be his last. By the actuarial tables he knows, perhaps, that his expectation of life at birth is almost three score and ten; but he knows something more precious than this: that there are moments when every part of the personality is mobilized into a single act or a single intuition, that they outweigh the contents of a whole tame lifetime. Those moments embrace eternity; and if they are fleeting, it is because men remain finite creatures whose days are measured.
— *Lewis Mumford* —

The rare moment is not the moment when there is something worth looking at but the moment when we are capable of seeing.
— *Joseph Wood Krutch* —

The vision comes and goes, mostly goes, but I live for it, for the moment when the mountains open and a new light roars in spate through the crack, and the mountains slam.
— *Annie Dillard* —

Engulfed by such splendor, I am plucked out of myself like a hermit crab from his borrowed shell and left stranded, naked and unfinished, on the sands.
— *Robert Finch* —

Do you not catch it? A something beyond sound, beyond sight, a measured beat as though you felt the metronome of the universe? How often the nature lover has mentally turned and run when this came to him, directed his thoughts to the study of color or form, or to unraveling the mystery of half-heard sounds. We fear the very fineness of spiritual experiences.

— *Sam Campbell* —

The sun was trembling now on the edge of the ridge. It was alive, almost fluid and pulsating, and as I watched it sink I thought that I could feel the earth turning from it, actually feel its rotation. Over all was the silence of the wilderness, that sense of oneness which comes only when there are no distracting sights or sounds, when we listen with inward ears and see with inward eyes, when we feel and are aware with our entire beings rather than our senses. I thought as I sat there of the ancient admonition, "Be still and know that I am God," and knew that without stillness there can be no knowing, without divorcement from outside influences man cannot know what spirit means.

— *Sigurd F. Olson* —

Life comes without warning.
— *Lieh Tzu* —

I screamed, and—lo!—Infinity
Came down and settled over me.
— *Edna St. Vincent Millay* —

The light died in the low clouds. Falling snow drank in the dusk. Shrouded in silence, the branches wrapped me in their peace. When the boundaries were erased, once again the wonder: that I exist.
— *Dag Hammarskjöld* —

Standing on the bare ground . . . all mean egotism vanishes. I become a transparent eyeball; I am nothing; I see all; the currents of the Universal Being circulate through me; I am part and parcel of God.
— *Ralph Waldo Emerson* —

That wind, that wind
Shakes my tipi, shakes my tipi,
And sings a song for me,
And sings a song for me.
— *A Kiowa song* —

Now you feel how nothing clings to you;
your vast shell reaches into endless space,
and there the rich, thick fluids rise and flow.
Illuminated in your infinite peace,
a billion stars go spinning through the night,
blazing high above your head.
But *in* you is the presence that
will be, when all the stars are dead.
— *Rainer Maria Rilke* —

When you are suddenly overwhelmed with a compassion that staggers you and you begin to run along the bank, at a moment when your fingers brush the soft skin of a deer-head orchid and you see the sun-drenched bears stretching in an open field like young men, you will know a loss of guile and that the journey has begun.
— *Barry Lopez* —

❖ GOD ❖

Incomprehensible? But because you cannot understand a thing, it does not cease to exist.
— *Blaise Pascal* —

When a mother cries to her sucking babe, "Come, O son, I
     am thy mother!"
Does the child answer, "O mother, show a proof
That I shall find comfort in taking thy milk"?
— *Jalal al-Din Rumi* —

God speaks to men and women in the clouds on the mountaintops, in the roaring of the torrents, in the stark awfulness of the cliffs, in the dazzling splendor of the unmelting snow, in the sun that splashes the west with blood, in the wind that strips the trees bare. Nature lives by the breath of his omnipotence.
— *Contardo Ferrini* —

Earth's crammed with heaven,
And every common bush afire with God.
— *Elizabeth Barrett Browning* —

God does not die on the day when we cease to believe in a personal deity, but we die on the day when our lives cease to be illumined by the steady radiance, renewed daily, of a wonder, the source of which is beyond all reason.
— *Dag Hammarskjöld* —

Whatever it is that hurls planets and instills faith is at the helm: and the goal seems to be nothing less than transformation.
— *Diana Kappel-Smith* —

Know first, the heaven, the earth, the main,
The man's pale orb, the starry train,
    Are nourished by a soul,
A bright intelligence, whose flame
Glows in each member of the frame,
    And stirs the mighty whole.
— *Virgil* —

When I was ten years of age I looked at the land and the rivers, the sky above, and the animals around me and could not fail to realize that they were made by some great power.
— *Tatanka-ohitika, a Sioux medicine man* —

If we could really conceive God we could no longer believe in Him because our representation, being human, would inspire us with doubts . . . It is not the image we create of God which proves God. It is the effort we make to create this image.
— *Pierre Lecomte dü Nouy* —

It could be that God has not absconded but spread, as our vision and understanding of the universe have spread, to a fabric of spirit and sense so grand and subtle, so powerful in a new way, that we can only feel blindly of its hem.
— *Annie Dillard* —

One of the greatest favors bestowed on the soul transiently in this life is to enable it to see so distinctly and to feel so proudly that it cannot comprehend God at all. These souls are herein somewhat like the saints in heaven, where they who know Him most perfectly perceive most clearly that He is infinitely incomprehensible; for those who have the less clear vision do not perceive so clearly as do these others how greatly He transcends their vision.
— *St. John of the Cross* —

The extreme of human knowledge of God is to know that we do not know God.
— *St. Thomas Aquinas* —

The knower and the known are one. Simple people imagine that they should see God, as if He stood there and they here. This is not so. God and I, we are one in knowledge.
— *Meister Eckhart* —

When you close your doors, and make darkness within, remember never to say that you are alone, for you are not alone; nay, God is within you, and your genius is within. And what need have they of light to see where you are going?
— *Epictetus* —

The good shepherds . . . have all faded into the darkness of history. One of them, however, left a cryptic message: "My doctrine is not mine but his that sent me." Even in the time of unbelieving this carries a warning. For He that sent may still be couched in the body of man awaiting the end of the story.
— *Loren Eiseley* —

For the religious mind and soul, the issue has never been the *existence* of God but the *importance* of God, the difference that God makes in the way we live. To believe that God exists the way you believe that the South Pole exists, though you have never seen either one, to believe in the reality of God the way you believe in the Pythagorean theorem, as an accurate abstract statement that does not really affect your daily life, is not a religious stance. A God who exists but does not matter, who does not make a difference in the way you live, might as well not exist . . . The issue is what kind of people we become when we attach ourselves to God.
— *Harold Kushner* —

A drunken man who falls out of a cart, though he may suffer, does not die. His bones are the same as other people's; but he meets his accident in a different way. His spirit is in a condition of security. He is not conscious of falling out of it. Ideas of life, death, fear and the like cannot penetrate his breast; and so he does not suffer from contact with objective existence. If such security is to be got from wine, how much more is it to be got from God?

— Chuang Tzu —

Though I did not get God, I got something. I got proof, if I may put it this way, of the existence of Man—which is doubted rather more often nowadays than the existence of God was doubted in Wordsworth's time.

— Joseph Wood Krutch —

As the marsh-hen secretly builds on the watery sod,
Behold I will build me a nest on the greatness of God:
I will fly in the greatness of God as the marsh-hen flies
In the freedom that fills all the space 'twixt the marsh and the skies:
By so many roots as the marsh-grass sends in the sod
I will heartily lay me a-hold on the greatness of God:
Oh, like to the greatness of God is the greatness within
The range of the marshes, the liberal marshes of Glynn.

— Sidney Lanier —

ACKNOWLEDGMENTS

Acknowledgment is gratefully made to the following sources for text used in *The Wilderness Companion*:

From *Tatanga Mani: Walking Buffalo of the Stonies* by Grant MacEwan © 1969, M.J. Hurtig, Ltd.

From *The Selected Works of Mahatma Ghandi* by M. K. Ghandi © 1968, Navajivan Publishing House. Reprinted by permission of Navajivan Trust.

From *Tramping With a Poet in the Rockies* by Stephen Graham © 1922, D. Appleton and Company.

From *River Notes: The Dance of the Herons* by Barry Lopez © 1979 courtesy Universal Press Syndicate/Andrews & McNeel.

From *The Outermost House* by Henry Beston © 1928, 1949, 1956 by the author, reprinted by permission of Henry Holt and Company, Inc.

From *Desert Solitaire* by Edward Abbey © 1968, McGraw-Hill, reprinted courtesy Don Congdon Associates.

From *Pilgrim at Tinker Creek* by Annie Dillard © 1974 by the author, reprinted by permission of HarperCollins Publishers.

From *The Land of Journey's Ending* by Mary Austin © 1924, The Century Company.

Crowfoot, Blackfoot leader, quoted in *Canadian Portraits: Brant, Crowfoot, Oronhyatekha, Famous Indians* by Ethel Brant Monture © 1960, reprinted by permission of Stoddart Publishing, Don Mills, Ontario.

From *Ideas and Opinions* by Albert Einstein © 1954, courtesy Crown Publishing Group.

From *A Walk Through the Year* by Edwin Way Teale © 1978, Dodd, Mead & Co.

From *Journey Into Summer* by Edwin Way Teale © 1960, Dodd, Mead & Co.

From *The Best of Robert Service* by Robert Service © 1907, 1953, Dodd, Mead & Co.

From *Conjectures of a Guilty Bystander* by Thomas Merton © 1966 by The Abbey of Gethsemani. Used by permission of Doubleday, a division of Bantam Doubleday Dell Publishing Group, Inc.

From *Lifesigns* by Henri J.M. Nouwen © 1986 by Henri J.M. Nouwen. Used by permission of Doubleday, a division of Bantam Doubleday Dell Publishing Group, Inc.

From *Straw for the Fire: From the Notebooks of Theodore Roethke* by Theodore Roethke, selected and arranged by David Wagener © 1972 by Beatrice Roethke. Used by permission of Doubleday, a division of Bantam Doubleday Dell Publishing Group, Inc.

From *Walden West* by August Derleth © 1961, by Duell, Sloan and Pearce, Inc.

From *The Sign of Jonas* by Thomas Merton © 1953, by The Abbey of Our Lady of Gethsemani and renewed 1981 by the Trustees of the Merton Legacy Estate, reprinted by permission of Harcourt Brace Jovanovich, Inc.

From *The Conduct of Life* by Lewis Mumford © 1951 and renewed 1979 by Lewis Mumford, reprinted by permission of Harcourt Brace Jovanovich, Inc.

From *The Unexpected Universe* by Loren Eiseley © 1969 Harcourt Brace Jovanovich, Publishers.

From *Collected Poems* by Edna St. Vincent Millay © 1956 Harper and Row, rights controlled by Estate of Edna St. Vincent Millay.

From *The Divine Milieu: An Essay on the Interior Life* by Pierre Teilhard de Chardin © 1960, HarperCollins Publishers.

From *Religion Without Revelation* by Julian Huxley © 1957, rights controlled by The Peters, Fraser and Dunlop Group, London.

From *The Perennial Philosophy* by Aldous Huxley © 1945, HarperCollins Publishers.

From *Selected Poems* by John Masefield © 1978, William Heinemann Ltd., London.

From *The Land of Little Rain* by Mary Austen, photos by Ansel Adams.

Ohiyesa, Santee Dakota doctor, quoted in *The Soul of the Indian* by Charles Alexander Eastman.

From *Land of the Spotted Eagle* by Chief Luther Standing Bear © 1933, rights controlled by Mr. Geoffrey M. Standing Bear.